Good text to use for ~~brief~~ course on _God_
Man
Ash

'Dialogue with Destiny'

FAITH AND ITS DIFFICULTIES

FAITH

AND ITS

DIFFICULTIES

by

DR. J. H. BAVINCK

PROFESSOR OF MISSIONS
AT THE FREE UNIVERSITY OF AMSTERDAM

TRANSLATED FROM THE DUTCH BY
WM. B. EERDMANS SR.

Wm. B. Eerdmans Publishing Co.
Grand Rapids, Michigan

© WM. B. EERDMANS PUBLISHING CO. 1959

L. C. Catalog Card Number, 59-8745
Printed in the United States of America
First printing, January 1959

The pieces here translated are taken
from the symposium *Het Geloof en Zijn
Moeilijkheden* by J. H. Bavinck,
J. de Groot, and M. J. A. de Vrijer, and
published by arrangement with
N. V. Gebr, Zomer en Keunings Uitgeversmij,
Wageningen, The Netherlands.

CONTENTS

I THE UNKNOWN GOD   9

  The Dialogue   12

  The Unknown God   15

  The Escape   17

  God in Christ   22

  The Neutral World   27

II MAN: THE ENIGMA   33

  The Labyrinth of Contrapositions   36

  Hopeful Daydreams   39

  How God Sees Us   44

  Faith and Its Difficulties   49

  The Solution   55

III THE CALL FOR DELIVERANCE   61

  The State of Befuddlement   64

  What Jesus Has Promised   67

  Repentance   79

THE UNKNOWN GOD

The Dialogue
The Unknown God
The Escape
God in Christ
The Neutral World

1

THE UNKNOWN GOD

One is possessed with a feeling of awe when one begins to talk about God.

Even when I talk with a friend about my fellow man, who has the same peculiarities and weaknesses that I have, I realize that at any moment I run the danger of doing him an injustice. It is possible that I will give the words and the deeds of my fellow man the wrong interpretation, that I will attribute ulterior motives, while in reality there are none.

How much more are we constrained by fear and dread when we venture to talk about God, whose thoughts we cannot think after Him, and whose motives we cannot fathom or understand. In advance I know that in everything I will say about Him, I will come far short in doing justice to His greatness and holiness. I know that in every thought I express about Him I will run the danger of pulling Him down to the *niveau* of my own life and thought. I am convinced that "no language has the word power adequately to express the ineffable majesty of His Being."

We wish to speak about the Unknown God. This does not mean that there is no way by which we may learn to know Him. From the clouds and the darkness which are around His throne, the Eternal Father has come down to us in Jesus Christ, and in Christ we see the Father. But it does mean that for very many of our generation He is nothing else but the UNKNOWN. And it also means that countless people who know Him or imagine to know Him, show in their daily life and walk and practice that in reality He is to them still the UNKNOWN.

There are three ways in which a small and mortal creature will in his life come in touch with God.

First there is the world of nature which surrounds us. From nature's overwhelming greatness one would think that man would acknowledge the existence of God directly and spontaneously, without any logical demonstrations and carefully built conclusions.

Every man who looks at the world with an open eye and an open heart, and is overwhelmed in beholding the mighty wonder of God's creation, irresistibly and without a shadow of a doubt feels himself forced to confess that there must be SOMETHING, that there must be ONE, out of whom all that splendor came into being. And that ONE, whom we call God, we meet in the immensity of nature.

Nature in itself is an unfathomable riddle. It does not distinguish between good and evil. The sun shines over the good and the evil. And the rain falls upon the righteous and the unrighteous. That God of nature is for us the Unknown God.

The *second* way in which every man on earth meets God is the way of guidance and direction. There are good days and bad days. There are all kinds of situations and circumstances, and in all these things the great Ruler of our lives speaks to us. Not to you and me alone, but also to other people, and in the history of races and peoples. The God whom we meet in all this leading and guiding

Does he mean the forcethat controls our personal history?

I would like to call the Regent of our life. However, the leading and the guiding which is given to all of us in our lives is an unfathomable mystery, the thoughts and purposes of which we are not able to unravel. The Regent of our life, He is to us the Unknown God.

The *third* way in which we meet God is the way of His revelation in Jesus Christ.

The great difficulty which confronts us in our life of faith is this, that we must see these three ways conjoin or merge as one. For we must understand that the God of nature, who gave life to the overwhelming multiplicity of suns and stars, is the same as the Regent of Life, who leads us and guides us, step by step. And we must realize that the Regent of our life, who holds all the movements of all that happens to us in His hands, is the same God as the God who was revealed to us in Jesus Christ. We must learn to understand that the *Unknown* God is the same as the *Known,* whose holy will for our salvation in Jesus Christ we behold. We must learn to understand that the Eternal Father, who created heaven and earth, which by His providence He rules and sustains, is *one* with the Son, our Lord Jesus Christ.

In the difficulty of merging these three ways as one, we experience stress, strain, tension. A secret lies here; we cannot find our way out with a few nice-sounding pious phrases and smooth, clever formulas. The tension reveals the stark tragedy of our time. We shudder at the appalling unknownness of God. What do we know of His plans for our distorted and mangled world?

In all the voices that reach my ear, in all the books I open, I recognize and see Him, the mighty Unknown, the Regent of Life, the Ruler of all nations. And with every step I take, I have difficulty understanding that the Unknown God is the same as the God who spoke to me in Jesus Christ. And sometimes I am oppressed with fear and anguish that I can see no confluence of these two, that I cannot see them proceeding in one direction, and that everything will be demolished and destroyed. That is our tension and our strain. And we shudder!

When we talk about the Unknown God, we shall not always be able to see a sharp delineation between the way of nature and the way of guidance and direction. These two often come together, and in both ways man confronts the Unknown. This riddle causes many worries and many depressing moods, and there is not one of us who can escape the stress and the strain and the tension of this mystery.

Denying—debating—defying Him. *Reacting against responding to*
Why so much words spend on arguing against god *if He isn't—it seems we're trying to whistle in the dark—to persuade our own conscience to get instinct of Him.*

THE DIALOGUE

It is my earnest conviction that, in his deepest hiding places, we can best understand man when we look at him from the point of view of a dialogue. And in that dialogue man is very much on the initiative. He thinks and he acts, he talks and he desires. From the fount of his inner self flows an endless stream of thoughts and desires.

Man's freedom

However, in that dialogue another also takes part: the mysterious OTHER, the One who holds the whole world in His hands, the One who rules and leads everything from moment to moment.

When God is absolutely sovereign

The Other — He is the One who determined the time and place of our birth, who created the milieu in which we saw the first light of life. He it is who defined the measure of our understanding, the strength of our body, our health and our ills, and the possibilities of our path of life. He met us at every step on the way, in ups and

downs, in sunshine and storm. In good and in bad days
He confronted us. He revealed Himself to us in many
other ways — but more about that thought later.

It was the mysterious Other whose power we could
never escape. He was always occupied with us, and never
left us to ourselves. And to His words and deeds we re-
acted. We began to dispute, oppose, and contradict. We,
too, got busy. And we did not resign ourselves to what
He did. We turned away from Him. We did not want
to listen. We did not stoop, nor bend. When He said
something, we retorted, and when He did something we
did something too. That peculiar dialogue between us
and the mysterious Other is what human life consists of.

This dialogue often comes to expression in very dramatic manner. I remember a confession which I heard
from a young man years ago. He told me of his college
days, and how devoted he had been to his studies. With
love and zeal he occupied himself with his work. He was
looking forward to a future of useful service, when his
father suddenly died. His mother was not able to continue to meet the cost of his education and was forced to
take him out of college and get him an office job.

"When that happened," the young man said, "I clenched
my teeth and I resolved to take out of life as much as
I could get."

At that moment the dramatic dialogue between the
Other, who rules all life, and the young man, with his
inner longings and tempestuous desires, had begun. The
Other had done something which was of great and decisive significance. It caused a turning point, and man
began to speak. And the words which he spoke were
words of revenge and anger and wrath. The first stage

of the drama of life had been set, and from then on there was only one important question in regard to life, namely, what course that dialogue would take and what the final outcome would be.

The young man I referred to was a person with a fierce temperament, full of energy, one who expected much of life. There are other men with less intense strains and tensions. Men differ in their reactions, and their sentiments are not always equally grim and dark and agitated. But the essence and the reality of life is this, that we can only discern and understand life when we think of it as a dialogue with the mysterious Other, who is hidden behind the mystery of life's happenings.

There are in our time schools of psychology that look at the deepest problem of life in a different way. There are those who think that the life of man can best be understood as a dialogue between the individual and the community. Man as individual is faced with the question whether and to what extent he will give himself to the community. His attitude can be one of service to the community, or, as an asocial being he can grudgingly, and with bitterness, malice, and ill will, lose all interest in the community.

There are in our day other intellectuals who try to illuminate life by describing it as a dialogue between the desires and the passions which live and agitate in man, and the power of his reason and will.

Though all of these views may contain some truth, it is my conviction that they do not fathom the sense and the meaning of the deepest truths. The dominating motive in the great drama of man's life is his concern with the Other who meets him in every situation of life.

THE UNKNOWN GOD

If it is true that the pith and the core of our life is determined by that mysterious conversation which we have from day to day with the OTHER, the UNKNOWN, then it is of the greatest importance that we seriously ponder who the Other is. And this will face us with the great problem of the Unknown God.

When I mention that name — the Unknown God — our thoughts invariably go back to what happened centuries ago in Athens. The Bible tells us that the Apostle Paul passed around the temples and the places of sacrifice in that pagan city, and that all of a sudden his eye fell on an altar with the significant inscription "TO THE UNKNOWN GOD."

When Paul stood before that altar he must have thought that it expressed in a terrifyingly real manner the tragedy of paganism. There is in man an ineradicable intuition that there exists a Higher Being, a God, and that this God is concerned about his life. There is in him a realization that this blind and dazzled world with its whirl of tragic happenings forms an impenetrable curtain, behind which is concealed the mystery of God's majesty. There is in man a vague sense of his own dependence on this invisible Power. He cannot grasp it, but he feels an impulse to seek it and to worship it.

Paul's thoughts must have been along such lines when he stood before the altar of the Unknown God. And these thoughts afford us a glimpse of a grave phenomenon. In paganism we often find the delusion of knowing things well. The teachers of paganism tell us all kinds of stories of gods and demons. They know their names and their histories. They create all kinds of peculiar happenings, which are often told in great detail, and they

imagine that they know their gods.   In short, they live
under a delusion of *knowing,* and their attitude is ac-
cordingly.

Alas, when such paganism becomes less sure of itself;
when its adherents become honest with themselves; when
at a given moment of real sincerity they reflect on what
they think and do! Then their hearts become heavy, and
doubts becloud their minds, and a feeling of distress takes
hold of them, realizing as they do that they are worship-
ping the Unknown. They begin to realize that all these
old tales were inventions; that they tried to cover the
unfathomable abyss of the Unknown with the leaves and
the branches of human fantasies. They begin to understand that man was engaged in deceiving himself by filling
the emptiness of his ignorance with human dreams and
thoughts. And when the blindfold is pulled off the eyes,
they see the grating wound and the bitter grief which had
caused them to suffer all those years. And they find
themselves standing with empty hands before the ornate
altar of the Unknown God. The intuition that there is
a God remains. But that intuition has lost its hold, has
no real content any more, is just a grasp in the infinite.

This altar to the Unknown God has stood in the history of the human race until this very day. It tells at all
times and in all places the same story, namely, the story
of a disillusioned paganism and of those from whose eyes
the blindfold of delusion is pulled off. Wherever men
have worshipped idols and false gods, there sooner or
later are born gnawing doubts and pangs of conscience.
Man comes to realize that, notwithstanding all thoughts
and dreams, one remains confronted by the Unknown,
who exists but whom our eyes cannot see.

A man can stand with different attitudes before the

curtain which hides the Unknown Other. He can stand there seeking and entreating, trying to fathom some of the mysteries which confound him. He can stand there in mute silence, quietly resigned to the fact that the mystery will never be solved. He can stand there with clenched fists because of the terrible fact that he does not know with whom he has to do. He can stand there scoffing and mocking in bitter derision and scornful laughter over the vanity of his own folly. But he can also stand there with great doubt in his heart, wondering whether behind that veil there really is Someone, or whether a hard and impersonal fate controls his life. That intuition, deep and indestructible, remains in his very being.

Life continues to be, notwithstanding all transformations, a dialogue with the mysterious Unknown, whose existence we can deny, but whom we can never wholly banish and expel from our thoughts.

THE ESCAPE

There are many ways to escape the painfulness of this dialogue, and I am sure that down the centuries man has tried them all. Presently we shall discuss what Christ has to say about this dialogue, but before we go to Him and hear His words, we will consider the many attempts man has made to find an escape out of the great difficulty of this dialogue with the Unknown One.

I think of the many people who in different ways imagined to have discovered the features of the Unknown in nature. They lifted their eyes on high, to the stars above, which night after night follow their quiet and wonderful rotation past the dark meridian. They looked at trees and shrubs and plants, which in promiscuous opulence arise out of the life-giving earth. They gazed at the waste and the wilderness of the desert, and they listened to the monotonous song of the sea.

They made a survey of all nature and said: "That is God." He is not here, or there, but He is the all-embracing All. He lives in every flower. And every tree which has sunk its roots into the nutritious earth, vibrating and quivering with the mysterious rustling of life, is a little of God. God is in the indestructible magnetism by which the atoms tenaciously hold on to each other, and by which the rotating suns lead each other in orderly orbit.

In that infinite, all-embracing universe, all contrapositions fade away, and all arguments and disagreements became vague and blurred. God is in the light and in the glory of the new day, but He also is in the darkness of the night. The fallen leaves in the forest form the new layers of earth, from which all sprouting green obtains its sap and juice — life out of death, and death out of life. And in the succession of nights, of light and shadow, and of death and life is the voice of the Unknown, the voice of God.

One who has looked at the world in this way, has at the same time looked altogether differently at himself. He realizes that he is nothing more than a very small and insignificant little atom in a great and endless infinity. The same force and drive of life moves through his veins, and his lungs inhale the same air which other people take in. He is assimilated in that great mosaic which we call the world. He is a very tiny piece of it, perhaps better looking and with more depth than other fragments, but in essence not more than they. He feels his own life fade away when he views it against the fullness of the universe. There seems to be no intimacy any more. The same magnetic powers of attraction and repulsion that actuate lifeless things and which take shape in plant and animal are the very same powers which also find their new forms in man, and he is nothing but just a speck in that great body; nothing but a tiny wave in a great ocean.

Another discovery man makes is that the norms of good and evil change; they lose their edge and their authority, because the Other with whom man has to do is none else but the All. There is no longer a powerful law which comes from the outside and makes demands and claims on him. For nature, of which he is a part, does not know any good or evil! The grazing sheep does not know that she destroys life with every tug and pull. Nature only knows the change and the rhythmic interplay of light and shadow.

If I am a part of that nature, then there is nothing in me but the compulsion of that life; the coercion to maintain my place and position in that life, until one who is stronger than I am destroys me and lives out of my death. Then the encirclement of the law is broken, and what remains is nothing but the restraint inherent in my own nature.

After this follows the greatest discovery, because now life is no longer a dialogue but a monologue. There is now no Other who talks to me and to whom I talk. The Other is none but myself, and my life has become a monologue with my own being, with the power of the divine which now is embodied in me

And thus the character and the meaning of life is attacked. Life loses its most essential character and mark of identification; it loses the character of the dialogue. There is no one to whom man now can speak; he stands alone, encircled on every side by surrounding nature, of which he himself is but a small and insignificant part.

When life loses the character of the dialogue, man, in the trying moments of his life, stands alone, without any help. In times of real need, in times when everything around him threatens to ruin him, he can find no way out. He loses all hold on himself when terrible temptations pull and fling and throw him down. There is no vision to attain, no course to follow, no goal to reach, no aim to achieve any more. And that is man in the utter helplessness of his lonesomeness. When the Other disappears, who speaks with him, and with whom he can and should speak, life loses all of its value and meaning.

There have been times in the history of mankind when all these things became painful experiences, and they have become especially real and painful in our own time. The question concerning the Unknown has become more actual than ever before. The question whether life is a meaningful and harmonious dialogue or a mad and an insane monologue, is a matter of great concern to many minds and hearts today.

There are those who simply ignore the Unknown altogether and omit Him from their life and thoughts; who ascribe the meaning and the background of all happenings to a blind law of nature or an inevitable fate. Others see the divine in human reasoning and reduce their thinking to an inner conflict within man himself. However, in that same moment the pith of life, that which makes life life, has been destroyed. The heavens still arch high above us, but there is no God any more to whom we can entrust our hearts in unbounded and all-embracing trust.

All these imaginations, no matter how visionary and idealistic they may be, are nothing else than a flight and an escape. They are a flight from any allegiance to God.

They take the most essential things out of life. They overthrow the altar to the Unknown God, and in its place they set up a mirror in which restless and wrestling man sees and worships himself. I am the Unknown. In my search for the Unknown God I have found myself, and the moment I live for myself, and follow my own will, I have found the Unknown.

I am the captain of my soul. — *William Ernest Henley*

I am a God in the deepest of my thoughts. — *Willem Kloos*

Now that the crisis of war has staggered and shaken all of Europe in its deepest foundations, all these things face us with appalling and terrifying clearness. I believe I am not exaggerating when I say that this inescapable and unsolvable enigma of the Unknown God lies at the very bottom of our confused and agitated time.

Two facts become more clear to us every day.

When we human beings with our limited horizon and understanding and egoism try to read the face of the Unknown in the splendor of nature, we become confused. The image fades and becomes blurred, and we are inclined to think that the All is God, and that we are little sparks of that All and therefore little rays and reflections of God. When that happens, the dialogue is stifled and choked and put to an end.

Secondly, when we human beings in the directions and the experiences of our personal and national life try to recognize the face of the Unknown, we become confused. We are inclined to deify our inner life and inner feelings, and to establish our own norm and criterion, and the Unknown becomes ever more vague, distant, and remote. The mirror takes the place of the altar, and gradually the dialogue comes to a stop.

Under the pressure of these two facts we are again faced with the mystery which those of ancient Athens gave such a sharp formulation: Who is the Unknown? How can we approach Him and how can we come in direct contact with Him, and have an intimate talk with Him? How can our life become what in its deepest meaning it should be?

GOD IN CHRIST

In the midst of all these questions we open the Bible and we read that the Unknown God has become known, and that He has spoken to us in Jesus Christ. After centuries of preparation through prophecy He has appeared in this world of ours. In Christ we see the very eyes of God. The curtain has been pushed aside, and God has come and visited His people.

The first thing that strikes us when we read the gospel of Christ is that in such a special way He became as one of us. He looked at the world with all its problems and riddles and it did not escape His eyes that "God maketh his sun to rise on the evil and the good, and sendeth rain on the just and on the unjust." In other words, no matter how beautiful this world may be, it still is, and in every respect, different from our conception of good and evil. It seems as if the cosmic system takes no account of justice and injustice, as if it takes an indifferent and neutral position in regard to the awful conflict between good and evil. And Christ was also aware of the fact that the great Regent of our lives, the God who leads us by His hand, sometimes seems altogether deaf to our entreaties and our lamentations.

Christ Himself in one of His parables pictured that Regent of our life as an "unjust judge," and to this He added that He was long-suffering and patient, and seemingly very slow to hear those who called upon Him. When Christ Himself entered the dreadful darkness, the most fearful and unfathomable abyss of His suffering, the same plaint and lament came from His lips, which once was uttered by man in his despair: "My God, my God, why hast thou forsaken me?"

In all these things Jesus Christ stands on "this side" of the curtain. He was not spared the grief and the riddle of the Unknown. He stared at it in the darkest depth of His suffering. "He . . . began to be greatly amazed, and sore troubled" (Mark 14:33).

In spite of all this, that same Jesus, who so perceptibly is one of us, is at the same time the One who came from above. He repeats it again and again that He and the Father are one, and that the Father performs His mighty work of salvation through Him.

This becomes very clear when we consider the light which Jesus sheds in all His teachings concerning the Unknown God. Our hearts become illumined with that light when we ponder the words He spoke.

We think first of all of that well-known parable of the Prodigal Son. The Prodigal left home and threw himself into the swirl and the swell of life. And in that far country he discovered that there, too, he had to do with the Unknown God, who even there controlled the goings of his life. For a time he became intoxicated with a life of sensual pleasure and was fascinated and bewitched by the glamour of this world. However, when his money was spent, there followed days of hunger and despair, and the dramatic dialogue with the Unknown began. All his friends deserted him, and he became a poor and lonely beggar. In order to exist he had to look for work, and the only occupation he could find was that of a swineherd,

Bavinck sees the Unknown = ? known god as one in this parable.

Here Barrick — ends "double image". on the screen—
the projector is "focused" — & the Unknown — : Known
become one.

24   FAITH AND ITS DIFFICULTIES

and that with a total stranger. This stranger happened
to be a disagreeable person who did not show any sympathy with the needs of his employees.

The young man tried to still his hunger with the husks
of the swine, because his scanty wages did not enable
him to buy sufficient food. But even that swill was denied
him. To be sure, the Unknown, the Regent of Life,
treated this young man very harshly. Misery upon misery!
And in the meantime sunset followed sunrise in its reg-
ular daily course. The blue and radiant sky shone in lus-
trous splendor over the green world. As time went on the
son became more and more impressed with the power of
the Unknown.

Jesus also tells us what happened when this young man
came to repent and returned to his *home*. "But while he
was yet afar off, his father saw him, and was moved with
compassion, and ran, and fell on his neck, and kissed him"
(Luke 15:20).

Let us not forget that the great Unknown, who in that
far country piled grief and sorrow and suffering upon
this young man, is the same Person as the Father in the
parable. In that far country the young man was not for
one moment forgotten or abandoned by the Father. In
other words, the prodigal son saw God in two different
ways. He saw Him as the Unknown, in the way of blow
upon blow and riddle upon riddle. But that same God
met him when he approached home. The face of God
had changed. It now was another God. The Unknown
had become the Known.

Or had He? No, not the face of God had changed, but
the young man himself had changed. He had come home
down a different road, the way of humility and repentance.

In another parable Jesus defines the riddle even more sharply and more grimly. In Luke 20 He tells the story of a certain man who planted a vineyard and let it out to tenants. The owner of the vineyard appears in connection with what follows to be the Unknown. The tenants in this case are the Jews. The Unknown, who remains until the end in the background, sends servants to the tenants, that they should give them some of the fruit of the vineyard. Obviously, the deeper meaning here is that these servants are the prophets and all those who in the Name of God have gone forth to preach and to defend His honor and His rights.

When the time comes, the owner of the vineyard sends a servant to collect some fruit from the tenants. But the tenants beat him and send him away empty-handed. The Unknown now sends another servant, with no other authority, however, than the word of the Unknown. The servant does not come with any soldiers. He does not come with any visible signs of power. For results he must depend on the Unknown's word, and on His word alone. The tenants beat this second servant too, treat him shamefully, and send him away empty-handed.

Nothing has happened, and so a third servant is sent, and again there is no other sanction than the word and message of the Unknown. The great Unknown remains unknown, hid, and enveloped. And this third servant is also wounded and cast out.

Finally, the owner sends His Son, and even the Son receives no orders of any kind for exercising His authority, other than the word of the Unknown.

In this parable Jesus sketches in brief outline the great world-shaking problem: There are preachers in this world who come to the people and plead for conversion, but from the Sender they do not receive any sanctions. The great Unknown remains in the background. All depends on the Word. Until the end of time there will be no sanctions — no flashes of lightning, no earthquakes. During this dispensation man must depend upon the Word alone. The Unknown Ruler of the world remains in the background until the time when His day has come.

When I read the Gospels, it always impresses me how Jesus made clear, explained and illumined these problems to His disciples. Even the most difficult point, namely, the fact that nature does not in the least seem concerned about moral norms and that it assumes an attitude of complete neutrality over against the terrible and tragic moral war which rages in the world, He did not hide from them.

Albert Schweitzer, the well-known missionary-musician-philosopher, writes in one of his books that the God he sees in the world is different from the God of his own experience. "In the world He appears as an enigmatic miraculous, creative power, and in me (that is, in my conscience) He reveals Himself as moral will."

To the problem of the "neutrality" of creation, Jesus refers with the words we have already quoted, that God "maketh his sun to rise on the evil and the good, and sendeth rain on the just and the unjust."

When Jesus touches upon that point, however, He does not do that with the intention of casting doubts in our hearts concerning the justice and the righteousness of God's rule of the world. Rather, He uses it as an example of God's unfathomable perfection. God is so perfect and so consistent in His love that He not only bestows His favor upon those who serve Him, but also upon those who hate Him. In other words, Jesus places this matter on a much higher plane. In this mystery He makes us see the greatness of the Father.

However, all this to a certain extent is just a matter of secondary importance. The essential point of the gospel and of the preaching of the gospel is this, that God revealed His eternal and holy will of salvation through the Cross of Christ; that Christ through His suffering and death reconciled us with God, in order that in the crucified Lord and Savior we might see the great love of God toward us, if and when we become reconciled with Him. Christ, the great King of this world, from whom, through whom, and to whom are all things, stands in a certain sense as a beggar before the portal of our heart and bids us open and lift up our eyes unto Him. The great and awe-inspiring Unknown comes to us as the Known, who invites us to behold Him as the Father that He wants to be for us in Christ.

The Regent of the world who remains in the background is still the Unknown. But the moment Jesus enters the heart of man the Unknown appears to be no one else than the merciful Father who all the time had been waiting for His lost and wandering child.

THE NEUTRAL WORLD

I should not end this discussion without calling attention to the fact that Jesus also casts a special light on the "neutrality" of this world. First of all, He shows us that this neutrality is only a temporary phase.

In the time in which we live it may oppress us sometimes that in the midst of war and crime, of disaster and calamity, of hatred and bloodshed, the sun still rises and sets in its usual course, as if there were nothing wrong. But nature is beyond all human quarrels and disputes.

She takes no account of the war between faith and unbelief; of hatred against God and love for God. Jesus shows that it has to be this way. The terrible battle of the evil one against God we see outlined against a neutral background. Nature does not take sides. She only seems to smile at the conflict.

When we ask why that is so, Jesus shows us that in this world the only thing that matters is faith. We must believe in His Word. We must believe the servants of the great Owner upon their word, even without sanctions and without such visible signs as lightnings, earthquakes, tornadoes, and other natural calamities. We must believe these servants because they come to us in the Name of God, and because our conscience tells us that they are right.

If nature would mix in this conflict — if the palace of Caiaphas would have collapsed in the night of Jesus' condemnation, or if Pilate would have been struck dead in the midst of the hearing — faith would not be faith any more; faith would be no solid ground of the things we do not see. Then everyone would be forced to bend and give in. Then the facts would force us, against our will, to agree with God. Then the Kingdom of Heaven would be a realm of compulsion for everyone. Then the only and decisive thing — the call to faith and conversion — would disappear. *The Rule of the Kingdom now is faith, then sight.*

And so through all the centuries of world history there remain two aspects, namely, that the Unknown God who meets us in nature and in the experiences of our life seems to be a different Person or Being from the Father who comes to us from afar. And these two prove to be one and the same the moment I bend my knees at the Cross of Christ and see in Him the face of the Father.

Secondly, Jesus gives us also an altogether different look at nature. When we take a very close look at nature in the light of what Jesus shows us, then nature does not appear as neutral as we first thought it to be. Nature also preaches, and in her own way. *Jesus gives us a new look at nature* *2*

The flowers in the field all day long tell us of Him who never tires to care and provide for His creatures. The tiny mustard seed tells us a secret; the secret of something infinitesimally small which waxes great and strong. The birds, winging their way through the sky, have a message for us. The vine with its winding branches tells us a story. All that unmatched work of art in creation is in its deepest sense not neutral in discussion and disputation. And though its story may not be the most convincing, it does tell a story to everyone who is willing to hear.

When I have seen the Father in Christ, and have beheld nature in its incomparable beauty, then I realize that the God who meets me there, and who reveals Himself to me in all that promiscuous beauty, is the same Father who was awaiting me at the gate.

Even our experiences in life, in all their freakishness and capriciousness and variegation, are not neutral. It certainly is not true that the good meet with nothing but joy and prosperity, and the bad with nothing but misery and adversity. Often the opposite seems true. But when I have learned to bow my knee in humility before God in Christ, in the realization of my sinfulness and lost state, then these experiences take on a different aspect. When a messenger of Satan comes and a thorn is given me in the flesh to harass me, then I begin to realize that behind this all there is a purpose to keep me from being too elated (II Cor. 12:7-9). I begin to see that in all these whimsical and fitful happenings a definite plan is operating in my life. I realize that all those things are not as capricious as they first seemed to be. I begin to see certain definite lines and backgrounds of which I was not aware before.

And as I progress and learn to know my God better, and when I become used to His face, then I also realize that, when I take a good and long and penetrating look at Him, the Unknown, the Regent of Life, unveils to me the very same features the Father has, who has received me in Christ.

The God who sent hunger and loneliness, misery and poverty to the far country, first seemed to be an altogether different God from the Father who was waiting. But in His deepest essence He is the very same. I see, be it faint and vague, that there is a plan in all these things, very closely interwoven with the holy will of God for salvation, the God who reveals Himself to me in Christ. And, what is most important of all, Jesus shows us that the Unknown will not remain unknown forever; that the mystery which surrounds us as long as we see through a mirror darkly, will one day be solved; that the time will come when the curtain will drop, and we shall see face to face.

We return to the altar of Athens, the altar of the Unknown God. We have seen that some have replaced the altar with a mirror; and they have set themselves up in the place of the Unknown. We have seen that others have mocked and scoffed and in revolt have slandered and blasphemed that cruel Unknown who rules the world.

And what shall we do with the altar of the Unknown? Paul, confronting it in Athens, left it standing there, but on it he wrote: "Who became known to us in Christ Jesus."

MAN: THE ENIGMA

The Labyrinth of Contrapositions

Hopeful Daydreams

How God Sees Us

Faith and Its Difficulties

The Solution

2

MAN: THE ENIGMA

Of all beings on this earth, none is more puzzling, inconstant, and unfixed than man. Through the being which we call man so many threads run that there is not the faintest hope of ever untying them.

Sometimes we feel as if in the recesses of our heart there is a great feast going on, when processions of happy thoughts and imaginations fill us with joy and ecstasy. Then again our inner self is like a busy market place, dizzy with screaming and shouting voices that fill our ears with a whirl of raucous and deafening sounds. Again, it is as if our heart is a forest in the fall when incessant rain gushes upon the withering leaves. The monotonous drip of the rain, the bending of the branches, and the dropping of the yellowing leaves — all can give us a feeling of unspeakable sadness and melancholy, like a wailing and mournful dirge. And there are times when wind and storm rush through the soul, whip and lash the waves, beat and batter them with fierce and angry power, and our heart seems like a wild and turbulent sea with ever recurring swells.

Man! Who will ever fathom what is hidden in the deep places of his being?

There are moments when man can be really great. There are, for instance, the stories we have read of many sea captains who, when they were shipwrecked, remained to the very last moment at their post, until death swallowed them up. These stories fill us with great admiration, and we realize that man in critical circumstances has done and is doing great deeds of heroism and sacrifice. And think of the great men in the field of science, such as Pasteur and many others! When we read their biographies and see what they performed, with undying energy and often against great odds, for suffering mankind, we are amazed, and our hearts are filled with profound respect.

We do not, however, have to go to the well-known. When we look round about us, we see many women, mothers of large families, who in daily sacrifice and denial, and often under all sorts of hardships, devote themselves to the care and the needs of their children; and we see many others who take a real and deeply felt interest in the needs of others.

All of these wonderful things that live and move in the hearts of men are a source of great joy. Many times we are deeply impressed with the things we see, and then we may rightly say, How great is man!

Then again, in glaring contrast, we see man reveal himself in bestial behavior.

One evening, with some friends, we discussed a report that a Chinese band of robbers had raided a village and had behaved in a most hideous way. They had burned all the houses, robbed the people of everything that had any value, and sent all men, women, and children into slavery. With deep disgust and indignation we read and discussed these things. Then, of a sudden, our discussion came to an abrupt end when one in our midst asked the question: "Could we, every one of us, under certain circumstances be debased to such madness and insanity?"

I still remember how this question made us tremble and shudder. We all realized that under certain circumstances and conditions we should be capable of doing the same things. We realized that there are volcanoes of hatred, dislike, and aversion hidden in the human heart, which, at some tragic and unfortunate moment, can explode into insane cruelties.

What is man! Great, and at the same time unspeakably and infinitesimally small; stronger than all other creatures, and yet the most miserable and weakest of all. A heaven of order and intuition on the one hand, and a hell of chaos and terror on the other. He can be a hero of devotion to duty, and a despicable beast in his frenzy and cruelty; the most beautiful and pure, and the most abhorrent; now sublime, and then again more contemptible than any other creature that crawls on the face of the earth.

Do not tell me that I may not generalize; that I may not place all men in one category. Do not tell me man must be divided into two groups: noble and respectable men, and brute and inferior animals! —Not two kinds of men— But two men in each man

I do not believe that any more. I believe that in all the substantial, solid, and sterling men there exists the same chasm and abyss, and I believe that our present world gives us plenty of material to prove that. I believe that even in the meekest among men there is enough powder hidden which, in a general explosion, would make them beings without brake and bound.

What would men of old, who could hold such appealing and interesting discourses concerning the divine background of human life, say if for a moment they could look upon our modern world? Our fathers, who so firmly believed that man would rise to greater and more perfect stature and would grow better and better, if we only would build more schools — what would they say if they could read our daily papers now when the word "man" has acquired such a frightful and horrible sound?

THE LABYRINTH OF CONTRAPOSITIONS

It certainly is not our purpose to try to solve that great mystery — man, the enigma. We are more inclined to believe that no solution ever can be given, and that it would profit us very little if we had obtained a solution. The only thing we can do is to unravel a few threads from that inextricable web of human powers and tendencies, and try to shed some light on it.

Everyone, when he thinks about himself and talks to himself, now and then contraposes his reason to his heart or feelings. Our feelings, we say, tell us to do this or that, but our reason tells us something which is diametrically opposed. In general terms we mean that our heart, our feelings, incline to something good, or, at least, something that can be tolerated. It is easy to get along with a man who has a heart. To be gracious and cordial is a virtue.

When we look at the matter closely, however, it becomes evident that these feelings often consist of sudden impulses of pity, of a desire to help, and of friendliness and kindness. And over against these our reason acts as a protecting power and influence, a kind of self-protection, prompting us not to go to extremes in well-doing.

That is approximately the thread of the contraposition of reason and feeling.

When we scrutinize that little thread closely, we soon notice that in it there is involved much self-deception.

For the heart, that great and compassionate heart, is in reality not nearly as magnanimous as it seems. Apart from the fact that often the heart is more asleep than awake, it has very difficult and unpleasant qualities. In that heart circulate altogether different currents than the spontaneous impulses of love for one's neighbor and of willingness to help. We all may be thankful that it is impossible for others to take a peep into our heart, because, if that were possible, their respect for us would receive a real blow. We have played a bit of a game with that heart; we have put ourselves to sleep and have covered the abyss of our real self.

And what about reason? When man develops intelligence, this as a rule does not amount to much more than taking a firm stand for his deep-seated egoism, in calculated self-preservation. Behind that so-called intelligence hides a big piece of heart. Not, however, that magnanimous heart we have just discussed, but a very hideous heart of callousness and self-love. In other words, that little thread, which we often use and operate in order to explain the problems of life, is by close scrutiny a yarn of our own fantasy. It does not give us a true picture of the precarious situation of our existence.

True, there are contrapositions in man. They exist, however, in a different way than we express them in the terms "heart" and "reason." There is the contraposition that again and again we feel ourselves driven to association and intercourse with other people, because in our own inner self we feel lonely and miserable, but at the same time we establish and entrench ourselves in an ineradicable desire to retain our own identity, and do not make one move toward self-denial and self-humility. We are driven towards each other as herds of sheep, and we are sepa-

Conflicts in man

rated by the wedge of our egoism and obstinate self-love. We need each other, every moment, to make our life happy and joyous and meaningful; and yet we systematically keep each other ignorant concerning the deepest stirrings of our heart, because we all live for ourselves under the ban and the illusion of self-glorification.

That is one contraposition, grim and deep, a contraposition which gives human intercourse an emptiness and a vanity. *yes,*

There is still another contraposition, namely, the passion of an unchecked life of sensual lust and desire over against our sense of orderliness and our inner drive to respect our fellow men. Sometimes there rises in man the senseless desire to destroy all checks and brakes and to let himself go to seed in bestiality, to go down to the very gutter. On the other hand, he takes great care to see to it that his neighbor cannot find a single flaw in his life.

That is a contraposition which can have a very dramatic power and effect in the lives of many in our generation.

Then there is a third contraposition, namely, that of fear and cheerfulness. An ill-defined and cryptic fear can gnaw at the heart and dull the pretense and semblance of cheerfulness with which every morning man turns his face to the world. In bad dreams that fear can grip him as an unbearable grief which consumes and corrodes him inwardly. And the same man in all his misery and wretchedness can for years play a comedy of lighthearted unconcern. Fear for his undoing, fear that the small structure of his happiness may some day collapse, fear that the bestial potentialities which he knows are in him may some day bring him to the brink of ruin, fear of the future, fear of the pitiless discovery of his own insignificance, fear of death, and fear of God — all that dark and

We cannot explain man? How do we attempt to explain God whom we cannot see?

We only study Him thru effects — or man etc. then as though we interpret them

MAN: THE ENIGMA

somber fear which lives and hides in the inner man is covered with a pattern of banter and lightheartedness.

This is a contraposition which hangs threateningly as a dark fate over the lives of countless people in our day. Indeed, when we begin to pull all the little threads of the inextricable web which we call man, we stand before ever new contrapositions, and slowly but surely we begin to realize how hopeless is the attempt to decipher the riddle.

In this connection I remember a story which I once read. Man in all the complications of his being was compared to a parliament, in which there are many parties. In the tumult of debate and discussion the parties become bold and aggressive, and at a given time a certain leader seizes the president's chair. He takes the gavel and proclaims, "I am the government." It looks as if there are no parties any more, as if all legislative and executive power has been vested in himself. That story is an illustration of the fickleness and uncertainty of human life.

By the power of circumstances which leave us personally undone, and by the compelling force of the demands upon us, life to a certain extent is kept in stable balance. Seemingly, there is a certain uniformity and a fixed and steady pace in human affairs. However, when, as now, in the storms of world-shaking events all the anchors break loose, then we begin to realize the fierceness and the awfulness of all those powers, and we stand again before the inescapable riddle: What is man?

HOPEFUL DAYDREAMS

In the midst of his perplexity, man still has within him one inalienable thing, namely, *hope*. There are times of dejection and great despondency, but invariably the mood changes, and repose and confidence return, and again man flatters himself with hopeful expectations.

Upon closer scrutiny we observe that man, in the course of the ages, has built this hope on all kinds of considerations. At all times he has tried to reassure himself and find foundations upon which he can quietly continue to build for the future.

There have been those, and there still are, who cherish the illusion that, in the end, reason will be victorious over all those fickle and capricious contrapositions which are hidden in man's heart. The wild animal of desire — so the Greeks of old thought — eventually will be tamed by a sensible and sober insight. We realize that it is to our own advantage to live in peace with each other, and to allow each other room and space in this world. So why should we not eventually learn and practice this? The brute force of our hatred and our unscrupulous egoism must be held in bounds by reasonable deliberation. When clear thinking and calm reflection once break through, we will eventually find an equilibrium which will enable us to build and order life anew.

Such is the first ground upon which man bases his optimism.

And the next ground is not less solid and firm than the first. Man, so it is reasoned, is and always has been a social and egoistical being. His egoism makes him always and first of all think of himself and turn to himself, and his inner barrenness always drives him again into the arms of the community.

When life consists of these two forces, why should it not be possible to come to a reconciliation? If need be, man for a time could deny his ego in the interest of the community. But when he has learned this, and has realized that his ego must be secondary and the community must be of primary importance, he slowly on can get used to the new situation, and all his problems will be solved. It would seem advisable to make this experiment first of all within the scope of a nation. A way, however, should be found to apply these same principles to the common interest of all nations, to mankind in general.

Thus man weaves his threads of trust and confidence, and, notwithstanding all disappointments, he proceeds to give himself in delightful abandon to the beautiful and imaginary air castles of world peace and world brotherhood. And this he does not only in relation to himself and his fellow men, but in self-confidence he even sets his face and makes a stand when he considers his life in his relation to God. He is willing to admit that his heart is full of whimsical contrapositions and that his brain distills many an evil thought. But, facing God, he still has the secret confidence that his case is not as hopeless as some people would think. In his inner self he appears to be confident, and he covers the yawning precipice with seemingly beautiful imaginations of the good which he thinks is in him.

Man has indeed distorted himself in many curves and bends in order to maintain himself and to avoid being pushed into a corner of despair and humiliation. I think of the old Orientals who, when they meditated upon the nature of man, came to the conclusion that man is invested with many evil forces, but that deep within him slumbers the quiet "witness," who is aware of the motley play of passion and misery, but who is not of it, nor in it.

There is in man an onlooker who keeps himself out of the game and who refuses to be dragged along in the stream, and it is that onlooker in man who is not stained and defiled by all the filth which hinders us.

When we consider that man may be indulgent, we grant that he is a hodge-podge of wickedness, but at the same time we hold a silent reservation that there is something in man which is not of him. And then we think to have found a little island in the great ocean of life, to which, weary of conflict and combat, we can retreat, knowing that there we will find rest.

Sometimes I think that man imagines that his corporeality is to be blamed for all the misery to which he is exposed. He is a body, and that bodily condition and constitution gives him hunger and thirst, and causes sensual appetite and lust to vex and plague him day after day. That corporeality is the source of his weakness. He can try to elevate his thoughts to higher and nobler things, but the leaden weight of his sensuality constantly drags him down again. And viewing the matter thus, the misery seems justified: it really is not his fault that again and again he loses his way and goes astray in the labyrinth of desires and strivings which inwardly torment him. And even God can hardly take offense!

I reflect how man eagerly seizes the pretext that the circumstances under which he was born and raised are the cause of his deficiency. How can one be good in a civilization which is rotten to the core? In the years of our youth we drank the poison of hatred and bitterness. No wonder, now that we are older, we poison others! If we only had the opportunity, in a radical coup, to turn civilization upside down, then the future generations would of their own accord become better and purer.

Yes, we are all painfully aware that we are governed by a divine law, that we should not be as we are. There are, however, many ways to escape that awareness. There are many soothing ways and means which help us to harbor the thought that God will not deal with us too severely. For are we not human?

When the consciousness of guilt brings too much pressure upon us, we put ourselves at ease with religious flushes of joy, which after all and periodically well up in our life. Then we adorn ourselves with a mantle of piety and devotion to duty. We flatter ourselves with the thought that, after all, we have performed many good deeds and thought many good thoughts, yes, many times we have really thought of God and have even longed for Him. And we feel sorry for ourselves and begin to look upon ourselves as victims, who really desire to live much closer to God but who find it impossible to do so in this confused and disordered world.

We ponder and muse how many times we really and very seriously think about God, but then we duck away in the trenches of our piety in order to hide ourselves from the terror of God's judgment. Undoubtedly, we think, God will understand that we miserable creatures, notwithstanding all our good intentions, make mistakes, and that our best efforts come to grief. If ever the truth comes to be known, we think, it will become evident that through all that egoism and through all those insane delusions runs the golden thread of our piety and our desire to become better creatures.

We are dealing with Man, the Enigma. In his heart of hearts there is the discord and the dissension of fear and lightheartedness, of egoism and the desire for communion with others. His life oscillates between the poles of reasonable considerations and a chaotic desire to live

his life to the full. He is in every respect a being of
capricious contraposition. He is twisted and confused.
Notwithstanding all disappointments, he keeps hoping,
but all his efforts crumble to dust. He remains a prisoner
of his misery, but he still believes in his eventual victory.
He realizes the chasm of his inner confusion, but still
he reassures himself in the face of God.

How will he ever escape that inner discord? How
will he ever get the right outlook upon himself and upon
his life? Who will tell him who he really is, who he
should be, and how he can become that?

Greek sculpture presented us with Laocoon, twined
about with serpents. So stands man, entwined with the
breathtaking, all joy killing, and strangling riddles of
his own being.

HOW GOD SEES US

It is impossible to disentangle the threads of human
life from the inside. We now approach the borders of
all psychology. Psychology can unravel a few threads
from the entangled whole. It can open our eyes to the
ties and knots that keep the whole captive, but it can
never uncover and lay bare the deepest and most basic
grounds. Man in his self-judgment and opinion can never
arrive at the full objective truth. As judge of himself,
he can never pronounce the right sentence. Even in
the moments when he pronounces the most cruel judgment over himself, deep within himself he grins with
pride that he passed such a fine and true verdict upon
himself.

To form a just opinion, man should disengage himself
from all his own speculations and contemplations, and
be willing to listen to God. How does God see us?

What is God's verdict upon our life? Only faith in God's
Word can shed light on the motives of our conduct in life.
God has told us how He sees us. He has shown us His
keen insight into the condition of our heart, and the only
thing for us to do is to accept His verdict and opinon
in faith.

And that is the most difficult leap faith can take,
namely, that I have to surrender the most valuable thing
I possess, the verdict upon myself, and submit to the judgment of Him who knows the deep crevices and hiding
places of my life.

When we talk about the difficulties of faith, I believe that there lies the great difficulty, and I ask myself
whether we shall ever come to the point where we shall
turn away from our secret self-evaluation, and whether we
shall ever discard all restraint before the judgment that
God passes upon us. Faith really is nothing else but
the courageous decision that I will no more indulge in
self-contemplation and speculation. I will not try any
more to disentangle the riddle of man — of myself. I surrender entirely to God's opinion of me. I refuse to accept any other judgment of me than the judgment
that God declares. I will stand on the side of God without any reservation. I will listen to what He has to say,
and that will be decisive for me.

When we open the Bible with that earnest intention,
we make many remarkable discoveries. The first discovery
we make is that the good people in the Bible often perform very bad deeds, and that the bad people in the Bible
often perform very wonderful and noble deeds.

Abraham is a mighty man, a man of great faith and of
noble character, and yet sometimes he performs such horrible deeds that we shudder, and we see the other side
of his inner life. Ahab is a bad king, a coward and idol-

ater, and yet he has moments when he can say some fine things. And with that explodes the fairy tale that humanity is made up of two kinds, good and bad, noble and evil. Therefore it would be folly for me to count myself with the first group. I am just simply a human being, and that is all.

God does not tell us in His Book that there are two kinds of human beings. There is only one kind. The contraposition is altogether different than we had imagined. There is only one contraposition: the human being as he is in himself, and the human being as he by the grace of God can become. To express this in a practical way, the Biblical teaching concerning man comes down to this: to the extent that there is some good in man, it is only due to the fact that God has not left man to himself and that he is still the object of God's concern.

The second discovery we make is that the Bible teaches that man indeed is a mysterious and complicated being. The Bible says that the heart of man is crafty and cunning, and exclaims: "Who can know it?" There are unfathomable depths in man, which we ourselves cannot pierce and penetrate. We simply do not know what is going on in our own minds.

In regard to all these things, man must surrender to the omniscience of God. "Search me, O God, and know my heart" (Ps. 139:23). "The heart is deceitful above all things, and desperately wicked: who can know it?" (Jer. 17:9).

We may not, however, construe these words as describing a place of escape to which we with our thoughts of goodness in man can retreat. The unknowableness of man and the unfathomableness of his heart do not mean that deep down in his heart there still slumber noble and divine forces which can give newness to his life. For when Jesus deals with that heart, and shows us the things that proceed out of that heart, He tells us: "For out of the heart proceed evil thoughts, murders, adulteries, fornications, thefts, false witness, blasphemies" (Matt. 15:19). Jesus does not point to a single good and sound virtue to which we firmly could cling.

At one time Paul talks about himself. He does not try to formulate his own thoughts, but he talks about God's judgment of himself; and that judgment reads, "For I know that in me (that is, in my flesh) dwelleth no good thing" (Rom. 7:18). The words "that is, in my flesh" indicate that Paul does not make any reservations, as if outside of that flesh there still could be found some good. For the word "flesh" is nothing else but an indication of what man is in himself, without the grace of God. This is a very hard statement, and it is almost impossible to fathom its meaning. Concerning that great complex of forces and inclinations which we call man, a judgment is here pronounced in a few short words, which is final and conclusive.

Man lives in a world of contrapositions. He is lighthearted, superficial, but he is also full of fears. He is egocentric, but by invisible powers he is always driven again into the arms of the community. He is intellectual, full of sober deliberation, but at the same time chaotic and demonic. He is capable of great moral deeds and of faithfulness and self-sacrifice, even to the point of death, but he can also be cruel, mad, and insane.

Now the Bible takes that complex man in all his dimensions, with all his contrapositions, and rejects him as something in which there is not any good. This means that, according to the true measure, namely, the standard and criterion of God's holy will, all man's "virtue" is wiped out. And to the extent that there still is good in him, it is due to the fact that God does not leave man to his own design, but shows His concern over him.

It is unspeakably sad that man is in such a sorry plight. All hopeful dreams and attempts to maintain good appearances are erased. All idealism is completely destroyed with one blow, and man is abandoned to a most radical pessimism. If this is man's condition, what can we expect of man and of his history? Where must we get the courage to keep on living, if that is all that can be said of us? Here we stand at the boundary of all hope. Here every outlook for a better future and every possible solution is cut off at the roots.

The Bible does not leave us in the darkness of this terrible sentence. The Bible tells us many other things about man and things of an altogether different character. In spite of his fall and in spite of the complete darkness of his being, man still is the object of God's care. God is still concerned about him. Man is not entirely detached from God. And God often calls him and speaks to him. Man's life can only be understood from God's point of view.

The fact that there still are such strong and moral forces active in man, that there is a sense of right and wrong and of good and evil in him — this is evidence that God is still concerned about him. And in the midst stands Jesus Christ, in whom God speaks to us and pleads with us to surrender to Him, so that in the hopelessness of our miserable existence we may become partakers of His loving grace. The image and the portrait which the Bible gives us of man still shows a few beams of light from above.

We cannot solve the riddle of man when we abstract him from God. Only when we see his image in
God's light does it become clear and sharp. Where all
hope vanishes, where all expectations end, outside the
boundaries of our thoughts there begins a new hope,
a new foundation, and the conviction that there is a
God who comes to us every day and tells us that He
has no pleasure in our death but rather that we should
return to Him and live (Ezek. 18:23).

FAITH AND ITS DIFFICULTIES

When a person has accepted the gospel of Jesus Christ
and has surrendered to Him, that does not mean that all
difficulties have vanished away. When a man has taken
that step, the difficulties of faith begin to face him, and
often annoy him. Most of these difficulties are caused by
periodic deviations from the right path. Often man will
again fail to see himself in the right light, and will find
himself confused and entangled in false speculations and
contemplations.   *Even as a Chr.*

The riddle of man oppresses all of us much more than
we think. First, there is the bitter experience that our   *a.*
inner life still remains full of contrapositions, and that the
forces thereof control our entire inner life, even our most
sacred acts. Every moment I am faced with the pitfalls
of my own being. I pray, and in my prayer my heart is
really filled with a genuine surrender to God. I feel that
my prayer is a matter of the heart. The words of my
prayer come spontaneously from the heart and with strong
urgency. No sooner do I rise from my prayer than, for
a split moment, like lightning, the thought flashes through
my mind, "I did that very nicely."

That vexes and oppresses me. I know that prayer is

nothing but the grace of God. It is through Him alone that we may pray and can pray. And when I appropriate that grace of God and act as if it is due to my own goodness and piety, that is the most dreadful of all faith's experiences.

I hear that a friend, a fellow Christian, has fallen into a certain sin which, measured by human standards, we would call a very grievous offense. The moment this story is whisperingly told to a group of friends with whom I am spending an evening, I feel for a split moment that there is in my heart a swift flash of joy. Ah, he too! And I feel as though I seek to justify the boundless shortcomings of myself with the faults and the sins of others, and find in them some kind of support. Secretly and deep in my heart I am playing the same old act before God, adorning myself with the mistakes and sins of other people. And that I am subject to such feelings and realize that there is so little real and true Christian mercy and sympathy in me, causes me to despair of my own life.

I know that I am a sinner, and I have confessed that before God. I have acknowledged that I was conceived and born in sin, and that by nature I am inclined to hate God and my neighbor. I believe that, and I have learned to have no other desire but the grace of Jesus Christ and His Cross. When I attend church on Sunday and the minister preaches about the misery and the lost state of man, I wholeheartedly agree. When he explains in a clear and lucid way that man is lost and cannot save himself, then I readily consent. When, however, someone has the courage to call my attention to a fault in my character or admonishes me concerning some wrong I committed, I become angry and irritable. And the thing he mentions is only a trifle in comparison with the much greater shortcomings and faults of which I myself am conscious, but still it irritates me.

This oppresses me and makes me feel that all my pious talk about sin is just a show and a pretense, and that my heart really was never in it, nor part of it. I accept the truth, as long as I look at it from a distance, and as long as it is a matter of discussion, but when it becomes near and concrete, and my attention is called to a definite fault or sin of mine, I must have nothing of it and refuse to give ear to it.

I have experienced a time of glorious spiritual jubilation in my inner life. On my bed of sickness and in many trying circumstances the Lord was very near, and I realized more than ever before what God is able and willing to give to me and through me. That was some time ago, however, and since then I have again fallen back into the doldrums of everyday life. When I think back on that period of heartfelt affection and tenderness, I discover that I had become possessed with a sense of subtle self-complacency. And in retrospect I now understand why the Lord took that feeling of ecstasy away from me: He no longer wasted His blessings on a man who annexes those blessings unto himself in self-flattery and vainglory.

The fact that this is possible oppresses me, and gives me a feeling that there never can come anything really beautiful into my life; and that when it comes it is at once soiled and stained by these hidden inclinations of my heart. I have had days in my life when God was very close to me and I begged of Him: "Let it always be so, my God, and never forsake me!" However, life always drifted back again to the usual and the common and the old, and I now understand that God could not do differently, because those days of joy and ecstasy were poison for me. I was not worthy of them.

That is the pain and the torment in our life of faith. Not that I am a sinner. I know that and I acknowledge that. But that everything which God in His riches of grace gives me, becomes soiled as soon as it comes within the reaches of my life; that what He gives me in order to make me humble and grateful, I use to flatter my inner self — *that* is the terrible burden of my life with Him.

There is another experience which is apt to make us despondent. We know that even the most saintly, as long as they are in this life, have attained only a very elementary degree of complete obedience. And that this is so, as we experience day after day, should be reason enough for us to be concerned about these matters.

And now, first of all, I must say something about the sexual lusts of man. How many there are, even among the true believers, who daily groan under the yoke of these fleshly desires. I have heard it said, and I believe it to be true, that the majority of men, when sin is discussed and when they fully realize the meaning and content of that word, find their thoughts almost invariably led to their sin of sensual passion and filthy fantasies, and always drawn to the things they really despise. And the fact that we have to contend with this during our entire life is something that fills us with horror.

There are other things that disturb us. Sometimes we are disturbed by our egoism and our indifference to the grief and the afflictions of others. All over the modern world voices are raised of bitter revolt and rebellion, of a desire to overturn our entire civilization. We object to the cries and the demands of these radicals, and we have

reasons to do that. Still, sometimes the sad truth grips us
that we have failed miserably to sympathize with the
sufferings and the needs of these people who are filled
with such a fierce hatred against our modern society.

We hardly give a thought to how we would feel if we
experienced their suffering and want. Is it any wonder
that in so many cases these people in their misery and
poverty have become bitter and try to seek their welfare
and happiness in directions where it never is to be found?
Often we are too severe in our judgment and do not seem
to be moved at all by the suffering and the want that we
see all around us. We have concocted a set of principles
and a line of thought, and argue and philosophize much.
But now that we are faced with the terrible judgment that
hangs over and threatens our world, we become conscious
of the fact that our lack of interest and sympathy is to a
great extent to be blamed for the insanity that now pre-
vails. And all this makes us inwardly restless and un-
certain.

Our voice seems to have a hoarse and husky sound in
the world. For we see in how many things we have been
self-centered, even in the things that we imagined were
concerned with Jesus Christ and His Kingdom.

We Christians in the modern world are beginning to
realize that we, too, have been infected by what we see
round about us. We have become as avaricious as others,
and as hateful. We have become estranged from each
other through all kinds of feuds and misunderstandings,
as people round about us are estranged from each other
through selfishness and cruelty. And the great and mighty
figure of Jesus Christ, who always moved toward His
worst enemies with unfathomable mercy and with deep
sorrow over their miseries, slowly disappears before our
eyes. We do not recognize Him any more.

Now that the storms break loose over the Church and
over the entire world, we feel ourselves uneasy and inse-
cure. We just did not give it a thought that sometimes
behind a crude and raw word of blasphemy there can be
hid a deep inner longing for true and real worship and a
great disappointment that those who call themselves
Christians are, after all, in their daily walk of life no
different than other people. All these thoughts now disturb and oppress us more than we can say. We begin to
look at ourselves as riddles and fearfully ask ourselves
whether we have really been touched by God, or whether
this was just a figment of our own imagination.

We have discussed Man, the Enigma, but there is a
riddle which moves us more deeply still, namely, the
riddle *Christian.* We do not recognize ourselves any more.
We see in ourselves contradictions which we cannot
fathom. Everything in us is different from what we had
imagined it to be. More fearful than ever the problem
faces us: Who really are we? What, through Christ, has
come to us and has happened to us? Is that all actual,
warm, and living reality, or is it illusion, and pious and
camouflaged pride?

When we consider the difficulties of faith, we can
rest assured that most of these difficulties are vested in the
riddle which is man himself. We cannot unravel the web
of our inner life. Our own view is often hazy, and we lack
clearness of vision in regard to the great and essential
matters of our faith. They often are dim and vague, and
this is because we ourselves have not changed.

There are a great many people who seek and long and
thirst after faith in God, but who never get anywhere because they are discouraged and deterred by what they see
in other men. If the Bible were a book that told us of

worlds far away and demanded from us a blind faith, we could accept it without doubt. The Bible is, however, a book that deals with ourselves, that tells us who we are and who we are to be, and it tells us of the power from above that can enter our hearts.

But that power must become evident and true in our lives; it must be seen and felt. "When that power does not become visible, and I remain who I am and as I am, then either Christ is a lie or I am a lie." Then either *He* has not the power to change our lives, or *I* have not fully surrendered to Him.

And in that moment we again stand before the riddle of ourselves.

THE SOLUTION

There is a solution to the riddle, available to all disrupted and confused people of today; a solution for all those who have doubts about themselves and about God.

That solution is not to be found in big and boasting words, but in action and deeds. We can lift our eyes far above the tumultuous noise of this world. We can go to Him, and we can say to Him: "Here we are, O God, we Thy straying followers. We do not know ourselves any more, and we do not know the way. Everything Thou hast given us we have made ugly, and every blessing bestowed upon us we have stained and defiled. The tragedy of our times has aroused us, and we now realize that we have been asleep. In stark egoism we have turned to ourselves when others begged for our help. We have closed our eyes to the needs of this world and in apathy and hardheartedness we have locked ourselves in our own safe theories. We have not been merciful, as Thou art merciful. Our hearts have not been moved by pity as Thy heart is moved with compassion when Thou beholdest the sheep which have no shepherd.

"And now the storm has broken loose, and there is a great conflagration all around us, and we are conscious of the fact that we are at fault and have miserably failed. We do not know ourselves any more. A yawning precipice we now see in our inner being. We are near Thee and at the same time so far away from Thee. We are tossed and flung to and fro. We are beaten and battered. We have no hold on ourselves any more; we do not see ourselves as we really are. Our brain reels, and it makes us dizzy to see that everything is carried along in the whirlpool of these terrible happenings. Help us, O great Shepherd of our souls!"

And I know what He will tell us. High above everything I see His Cross, on which He carried the sins of the world. It is as if He tells us: "Do you understand it now? In your inner self you always had such a high opinion of yourself, and you depended on your own views and judgments. But now, with your life shattered in this wretched world, when all imagined securities fall away, you stand close to Me and My Cross. You now stand before the splendor of the inaccessible light of God's burning holiness, and in the enigmatic character of your inner being there is nothing left on which you can take hold. There is now none but Me. Believe in Me as your only Savior. I will save you. And now that everything has gone to pieces and you are quite broken and shattered, now my grace will be sufficient unto you."

I believe God has written these pages of history in order to make us small and very insignificant in the enigmatic character of our life. The Cross of my Savior alone is great. Let us bow, let us all bow together very deeply under the flaming judgment that sweeps across the world. All I imagined to have in myself, I have lost; it is vanished. The only thing I now see is the Cross of Him who reconciled me to my Father in heaven.

Is this all Christ will tell us? Does He not show us the way to the future? Does He not offer us deliverance from all the restlessness of our lives? Is there no way to escape from our fears and anxieties?

Yes, He tells us more. He also speaks of deliverance. He demands, however, that we first be still, that we first kneel before His Cross and embrace it as our only hope and security.

The Enigma — Man's dualism: conflict
— The Chr too

Solution: No confidence in the flesh — but rest in Xst alone.

THE CALL FOR DELIVERANCE

The State of Befuddlement
What Jesus Has Promised
Repentance

3

THE CALL FOR DELIVERANCE

There is in our modern world an urgent and continuous cry for deliverance, not from external things, such as disaster and adversity, but from the limitations of our own being, which is a deeper and far more human need for deliverance. Any number of people in our day realize that there has to come a change in their lives, if there is ever to be again a time of peace and harmony. And this distressed feeling fills people all over the world with a great longing for a new and moral rehabilitation.

Today we are conscious of the fact that demonic forces slumber and lie dormant in all of us. On the other hand, we also know that we possess gifts of sober and pregnant intellect. These, however, have not been of sufficient force and number to give us the peace and the security we so much desire.

But there is another force in man. There is in him a sense of morality, a conception of good and evil. And now we are irresistibly faced with the question whether we are able to cultivate and strengthen this moral urge. Are we able by training and education to convince our youth, who are growing up in a disorganized and shattered world, of the necessity to take a firm grip on the moral norms, the pre-eminence of which we still hold dear in the depths of our being, notwithstanding all our

wanderings and digressions? And are we able to do this
in a more effective way than we of the older generation
have done?

For the Christian Church this very moment is an opportunity of the greatest significance. The world around
us is not sure of itself any more, and it is more pre-
pared than before to acknowledge that it has failed. From
all sides the question is raised how we can build our life
anew, how we can acquire more stability in our acts, and
more sense and meaning in our endeavors.

The Church is entrusted with and committed to the
gospel, which speaks about the light burden and the easy
yoke by which tormented man can find rest. The Church
can propagate and spread the good news of salvation in
a confused world. She can tell of One who is mightier
than all the forces of sin, mightier than all the demonic
forces that threaten to overwhelm us, and who has the
power to renew our lives and to lift us up on high.

Man nowadays is aware of his egoism and realizes that
his ineradicable ego can be a curse. He yearns to become
more detached from himself. He understands that his
compulsive urge to be self-sufficient chokes all real enjoy-
ment of life. He realizes that sexual lusts and erotic desires, no matter how alluring they may seem, are in essence a curse. It does not escape him that the forces
within him are full of dreadful dangers and risks, and
that they obscure and darken his life. He has become
aware that love of money and desire for honor are un-
tamed monsters that can spur him on to great action and
risks, but which in the end make life hollow and deso-
late.

These thoughts are no longer concealed and ignored.
There are thousands of people who are conscious of them

and who are willing to admit them. In fact, there are many who feel that it is wrong to expect their neighbor to have a change of mind and heart; on the contrary, they believe that we should begin with ourselves. We ourselves, individually, must try to lay new foundations.

In a world that despairs of itself, it is a tremendous thing to speak about Jesus Christ, the Savior of men. It is a source of inexpressible joy that Jesus Christ is able indeed to deliver us from that deep-rooted egoism, and that He *will* do this and *is* doing it. And it is something that raises our Christian life to the highest intensity if we can say unhesitatingly that Jesus Christ really has the power to deliver us from all these sensual and erotic lusts and desires that weigh us down under a great burden of troubles and anxieties, and that He *will* do that and *is* doing it.

Moral rehabilitation is not a mere air castle or utopia. It is a real and living and tangible reality in Christ. He is willing to give deliverance to the dejected and depressed victims of the twentieth century. And if it ever were true, it is true here: There is no limit to the purchasing power of His righteousness nor to the greatness of His infinite and abiding love for the repentant sinner. It is a marvelous thing to bring this message in our day. There is, however, one condition, namely that we ourselves must believe it. We must have the assurance in our heart of hearts that these things are true, and that Jesus Christ can and will transform us from day to day.

A devout and true Christian once told me that nothing ever caused him more anxiety than the fact that he always remained the same. The most impressive sermon, one that really edified him greatly, did not change the alarming fact that he went home and remained the same person, with the same sins and the same shortcomings. The material of which our lives are made seems to be so cumbrous and so inflexible that even the severest blows cannot jar it.

Deliverance — is that a mere word, or is it a reality? Can Jesus Christ really be a power unto the renewing of my life, or am I destined to plod and trudge along as I am, until death? Here lies one of the most grievous and smarting problems in our Christian life.

THE STATE OF BEFUDDLEMENT

This problem we should ponder well. And to do this we should carefully rule out all pseudo-deliverance, that is, all the great movements in our lives that look like deliverance but do not prove to be such in reality.

In days of great strain and tension man may for a long time be relieved of things to which he often is subject, such as egoism, lust, love of money, and so forth, because in such days the heart is flooded by a single great emotion. For example, soldiers who go to war and who know that it is a question of life and death are in such a situation free from many of the normal tensions. The employer is no longer an employer. He marches next to his employee. They march and sing together, and both of them are aware that the great decision can come at any moment. All ties have been loosened. There is no place any longer for ambition and selfishness, because in sight of death all the common, everyday things in life have become relative. What is the use to bother about everyday worries and cares? They have blown away in the face of mortal danger. In the all-devouring emotion of the moment, new thoughts are born. Friendship, real and genuine friendship, yes, friendship unto death now can thrive, now that all securities have been wiped out and man is faced with the awesome reality which any moment can annihilate him.

During the First World War a long and furious battle raged before the French fortress of Verdun. Thousands upon thousands lost their lives in that struggle. From a soldier who had fought in that most terrible combat and had lost his right arm, I once heard the significant words: "Never did I feel myself closer to God than at Verdun."

Such a statement may surprise us for a moment, if we know the meaning and import of a modern battle, and still we can understand it. I can understand the wonder of a man when suddenly all evil desires, all weaknesses of character, all the small and insignificant things in his life have been obliterated, and when in every fiber of his being he is kindled to a powerful emotion. All the entrenchments and self-vindications of his life have been completely wiped out. He feels himself lifted to an entirely new sphere of life, where there is no place any longer for small quibblings and false illusions, because any moment, swift as lightning, he may encounter death.

All this, however, may only be a semblance of deliverance — deliverance of a moment's duration. When man returns home from the battle, then all the thousands of little threads that have entangled him suddenly return to him.

A person may experience the same thing on a sickbed. When the fever races through the blood, when one's heart is full of fitful thoughts, sometimes a smile of surprise is born concerning the sensations we then experience. How we were irritated and harassed by all kinds of worries about vain and trivial things! And now how infinitesimally small seem all those insane and worth-less things we were so concerned about yesterday! How radically different life suddenly becomes when one sees it in this perspective! That which seemed so important becomes small and insignificant, and the things that stirred us deeply become futilities and trifles. Sins that bothered and irritated us day after day suddenly disap-pear. And that is the most dangerous dream of deliver-ance in our sickness, namely, the illusion that we now are free from the restraints of our daily sinful life.

This dream, too, comes to an end. Everyone who has been ill knows that when health returns, one's heart is at once enveloped again in the web of the same desires in which it heretofore had been imprisoned.

Similar deliverances are possible at many times and in different forms. During a large meeting or conference, when something of mass suggestion steals through our souls, such a feeling of deliverance may become evident any moment. A fiery speech or argument or plea, a spontaneous and heart-rousing song, emotional en-thusiasm for a noble cause — these all have the power to obliterate the inhibitions that bind and fetter our lives. It seems that for a moment there is no sin, as if evil does not exist, and as if one may mock at its fetters.

Let us not forget, however, that such deliverance, no matter how hopeful it may seem, in its deepest mean-ing is nothing but an illusion. It is not genuine and not lasting. When we are thrown back on the everyday drudgery of life, we are fettered again with the same chains and shackles, and we see again the sneering shapes of all the mistakes and faults and defects that had kept us bound and in bondage before.

Man is such a mysterious being that sometimes he imagines that he can crawl out of his skin, and become a different being. But that which annoyed and irritated him before returns to vex him again. We can dream that with a bold blow and a strong jerk we can throw these defects off, but they are tough and tenacious. They remain with us, and in the most unaware moments they face us again.

We are not, however, here concerned with illusions of deliverance, but with real deliverance. We do not seek deliverance in sudden and tempestuous emotions, but what we seek is deliverance in the hard and sober and vital rule and practice of life.

And when we do that, the question faces us: Is it true that Jesus Christ can and is willing to deliver us from the yoke of all those faults and defects under which we have groaned for so many years? Is He really able to make us into different beings, so that the work of deliverance and redemption can be seen in us? Do we really believe that He has that miraculous power, or do we, tired of struggle and combat, resign ourselves to the ruts and grooves of the old life?

It would seem to me that we should not evade these questions. Our time clamors for an inner rehabilitation. In the strain and tension of our time we must be articulate, and we must freely and openly confess and proclaim what we may expect of Christ. But it is imperative that we ourselves believe in the deliverance He provides, and that we are serious about the matter.

WHAT JESUS HAS PROMISED

What we need more than ever in our time is to pause and quietly consider the things that Jesus has promised us. Since these promises concern the greatest question in life

— whether we really and truly can become different beings — the best way is to go straight to the Gospels and accept and assimilate every promise Christ has made.

The first thing that strikes us when we open the Bible is that we do not meet as many "changed" people as we had expected. This is due to the fact that it is not man who stands in the center of things, but Christ. The Gospels are concerned with Him and with Him alone, and what is said about man serves the purpose of showing us who *He* is and what *He* has done.

We must not forget that the Gospels take us back to a time full of tension, a time of great disturbances, when many relations were different from what they are now. This is evident from the fact that with reasonable ease people broke with home and with their affairs and went into the completely unknown when they followed Jesus from place to place. This fact lends to all the happenings which we read of in the Gospels a particular color; it would be impossible to transplant these events to our time and circumstances. We read of Matthew the tax collector. Jesus called him, and Matthew immediately takes a decisive step. He becomes a follower of Jesus. From a human point of view it would have been more interesting reading for us if Matthew would have remained a tax collector and if in that occupation he had lived and behaved according to the demands of Jesus. And how would a Christian tax collector have behaved? The Gospels do not tell us that.

They do tell us of another tax collector, Zacchaeus, who promised to give half of his possessions to the poor and to compensate for all that he had done wrong. The Gospels are silent, however, and would we not have liked to know! — as to how that turned out, whether Zacchaeus really did remain a tax collector, and what happened to him after he met Jesus.

To all these questions the Gospels do not give us an answer. But when we take a good look at the circle of Jesus' followers, it does not escape us that there were people among them who by the grace and the power of Jesus had been led to do and to perform great and mighty deeds. We see a Mary, who in simple and unobtrusive ways performs a deed of world-wide significance when she anoints Jesus in preparation for His passover. We observe the disciples, who leave and break with much that is dear to them out of sincere and unfeigned devotion.

These same disciples, however, also show us that in many things their hearts still were bound and fettered. Even they were still entwined in the web of jealousy and ambition, of self-centeredness and self-glorification — the same threads that enmesh our lives. Now and then it looks as if those threads do not hold and bind any longer, but they never completely unloosen themselves. Even long after Jesus has ascended into heaven something of the old spirit remains in the circle of the disciples. Think only of what Peter did in Antioch, how the love of honor got the best of him (Gal. 2:11-13)! Or think of the attitude of the Church Council in Jerusalem, against Paul. That attitude was not entirely fair and reasonable (Acts 21:17-25).

No, these men had not as yet been delivered in the full sense of the word. They still had the same inhibitions that bind and imprison us. Very plain indeed is the confession of one of them, namely Paul. He always writes in sober terms about the deliverance that came into his life by the power of Christ, but in the classical chapter of Romans 7 he tells us in deeply moving words of the inner discord of which he is always conscious: "For I delight in the law of God after the inward man: but I see a different law in my members, warring against the law of my mind, and bringing me into captivity under the law of sin which is in my members" (Rom. 7:22, 23). And then he finishes with the heart-rending cry for deliverance: "Wretched man that I am! who shall deliver me out of the body of this death?"

That same somber melody with its deep bass clef runs through all the letters of this courageous champion for God. In one place he writes about the resurrection from the dead and about becoming a new man in every respect, but he meekly and humbly concludes: "Not that I have already obtained, or am already made perfect; but I press on, if so be that I may lay hold on that for which also I was laid hold on by Christ Jesus" (Phil. 3:12).

No, Paul does not stand before us as a joyful perfectionist who with one tug wrenches himself loose from the old bonds of sin. He is altogether too honest, too realistic, and too humble. He knows very well that we can only stand against the temptations of the devil when we are "strong in the Lord, and in the strength of his might." And he further exhorts us: "Put on the whole armor of God, that ye may be able to stand against the wiles of the devil. For our wrestling is not against flesh and blood, but against the principalities, against the powers, against the world-rulers of this darkness, against the spiritual hosts of wickedness in the heavenly places" (Eph. 6:11, 12).

What a picture these words, written during the first century after Christ, present to us living today, almost two thousand years after they were spoken! One could not better and more vividly describe our present dilemma.

A German mystic of the Middle Ages once said of the struggle for deliverance that it cannot be obtained "by limp little jog trots," but that it is a matter "of daily wrestling" (Heinrich von Suso). And Paul, who had a deep realization of the precariousness of that struggle, with childlike optimism could say: "But we all, with unveiled face beholding as in a mirror the glory of the Lord, are transformed into the same image from glory to glory" (II Cor. 3:18). He discovers that he is growing in grace; that a change is taking place, be it slow and gradual; and that this change is a change into His likeness "from glory to glory."

There is, however, still much to be said. Thus far we have become convinced that the problem of deliverance as a real and lasting good cannot be solved with a turn of one's hand. We have also seen that a Christian is a being of many contradictions. And, above all, we have come to realize that there must be growth in the life of a Christian. There must come a change, be it slow and not always visible.

But until now we have not got very far. That is because we started from the wrong premises. Our beginning was from the practical point of view. We began with tangible realities, and, as it were, from the bottom up. We should have begun from a different starting point, namely, from the word of Christ Himself and from His promises. In other words, we should have begun from the top down.

What does Jesus say? That is the question that should concern us from now on.

And forthwith we notice a very significant thing, namely, that Jesus in the Sermon on the Mount speaks about a radical conversion and transformation as something self-evident. He clearly declares that in the Kingdom of Heaven everything becomes radically different. There is no place for hostile feelings towards one's neighbor, for adulterous desires, for revengeful feelings, for sanctimony and hypocrisy. There the new life grows and thrives as a self-evident fact. The Kingdom of Heaven in its very essence is diametrically opposed to the everyday course of life. There those who mourn are called blessed; the Kingdom of Heaven is for the poor in spirit; the "woe be to you" is for the rich.

The Kingdom is in every respect a miracle of God. It cannot be built by stained and polluted hands, but it descends from above, and then it lives and grows as a grain of seed in the heart of him who has received it. In our language we would say it is a dynamic thing. It does not rest until the dough is leavened. In this shattered world it has to grow amidst the weeds. In its essence, however, it cannot tolerate the weeds. It wants to fill all hearts.

The Sermon on the Mount in a general sense remains more in the sphere of a command than of a promise. It states and expresses the new, and demands that our hearts without any reservation embrace the new. But still it shows us relatively little of the background and does not reveal how and to what extent these things really can and will happen, and what place Christ takes in all these things.

In the parables we notice a change, inasmuch as there the stress upon command is not as strong and we are told in positive statement what is to happen. And there, too, we are impressed with the events that are in such great contrast to our daily experiences: The Kingdom of God grows like a tree, it yields sixty- and hundredfold fruit, it is bought with everything that is precious to man, it grows and we do not know how — and everything looks unusually self-evident and common. The Savior Himself calls these things "hidden things," of which the disciples get a mere glimpse and which are impossible for others to understand.

This mystery does not lie so much in the parables themselves, for in most cases they are as clear as crystal; rather, it lies herein, that all these seemingly quite obvious things are in most flagrant conflict with the tangible reality of our own everyday life. In the reality of life, as we see it, these things are not obvious. The Kingdom of Heaven often looks much more like a golden ornament locked up in a vault than like a seed in the field. Often it seems to bear no fruit at all, at least no visible fruit. Neither does it grow altogether by and of itself. And we ourselves do not know how it grows. In other words, the mystery of the parables is that all the phenomena which in our twisted and distorted lives have become countless problems, are obvious truths in the Kingdom of Heaven.

And with that an entirely different light is thrown on the matter, so that it now becomes clear that I must take care not to thwart and oppose. The Kingdom grows of itself, provided I do not obstruct that growth and lay no obstacles in the way. In the Kingdom, as in all the works of God in nature, lies a natural urge for expansion which, because of inner necessity, reveals itself in many and various ways.

Forthrightly and without mincing matters, Jesus discusses with the Jews in Jerusalem the question with which we are now concerned. To a small circle of people who believed in Him He spoke these significant words: "If ye abide in my word, then are ye truly my disciples; and ye shall know the truth, and the truth shall make you free" (John 8:31, 32).

These last words evidently were misunderstood by His listeners. They took them in the political and external sense, and they objected. Jesus then elucidated His teaching as follows: "Every one that committeth sin is the bondservant of sin . . . . If therefore the Son shall make you free, ye shall be free indeed" (John 8:34, 36).

In these words of Scripture Jesus tells us a few things that are of the greatest value for us. First of all, these words place full weight on the fact that sin means slavery. There is in sin a certain fatalism. It brings forth new and more sins. Every deed we perform, every thought we cherish cuts, as it were, a channel which in the future pulls the course of our life back to the same faults and mistakes of yesterday. And we are unable to disengage ourselves from these faults. Sin is a hard and cruel tyrant and makes all escape impossible.

We need not say much more about this. If there is one thing that is pitilessly verified every day of our lives, it is this: that there is a tyrannical power in our character sins, in our common, everyday sins, against which we can fight tooth and nail without ever wrestling ourselves free from their power. To be really free — which means not in a moment of enthusiasm to ignore these bonds, but to become really delivered and free from them — for that, man needs the help of the *Son*. The Son can really make us free. He can really deliver us from the pinching fetters of our own sins.

This power Christ has because He tells us the truth, because He is the truth, and because He practices the truth. "The truth shall make you free." That little phrase contains a world of thought. The truth! That is when I drop all illusions concerning myself and my life and I place myself on the foundation of God's Word and on what He tells me in His Word. It means that I fully acknowledge the reality of my own life, but also that I see the reality of God's love in Christ. In order to obtain deliverance I must abandon all imaginary supports and excuses and throw myself with complete abandon into the arms of truth. The great inner deliverance, the deliverance from my love of self, my egoism, my erotic desires, and the deliverance from the daily pressure, is only made possible by the truth. In fact, the truth, in and of itself, brings about a spontaneous deliverance.

In the Gospel of John we find another word of Jesus that has reference to the same thing. In chapter 5 we read of a man who had been paralyzed for many years. When Jesus approached him and saw that all hope for a cure had been extinguished from his eyes and that this man had not the least expectation any more for his mortal life, He addressed him with the words: "Wouldest thou be made whole?" In the conversation that follows it becomes very obvious that these words have a deeper meaning. Jesus sees the paralysis of this man as a sign of the inner paralysis which man suffers. These words show that in order to find deliverance, man must really desire to be delivered.

A sick person may sometimes baby himself to the point where he impedes and slows down the process of healing. This is much more true of the inner man. There must be a real and strong will at work. Man can sigh and complain under the pressure of his faults and sins, but inwardly he cherishes them and tenaciously holds on to them. Deliverance is possible only when there is a strong and serious desire to obtain it.

We find this truth illustrated in the history of the well-known Church Father, St. Augustine. At a certain point in his life he had come so far that he heard, as it were, the voice of God saying: "Awake ye that sleep, and arise from the dead." To this he answered: "Yes, by and by." Inwardly the thought remained alive, Augustine later confessed, that he preferred to sleep on for a while. "Convert me, O God, but not as yet." Later in life he clearly realized that in such a half-hearted and irresolute condition a man can not expect miracles. "To go," he then said, "means to be willing to go with strong and complete willingness [*fortiter en integre velle*], not to swing the half-wounded will to and fro" (*Confessions*, VIII, 5 and 8).

We hear the Savior speak about this matter in still another place, namely, in the very short parable in Luke 11:9-13. In that parable Jesus deals with prayer and explains that an earthly father would not be so cruel as to give a child a scorpion when he asks for an egg. With a significant leap of thought, which we so often find in the Gospels, the Savior then continues: "If ye then, being evil, know how to give good gifts unto your children, how much more shall your heavenly Father give the Holy Spirit to them that ask Him?"

In other words, when we believe in God's love in Jesus Christ and keep on worrying about all kinds of inner conflicts and difficulties, there is one thing we should do, namely, go to Him in full and unlimited faith and trust, and ask Him for the guidance, the direction, and the indwelling of the Holy Spirit. In Him there are immeasurable sources of great power for our use.

There is nothing God would rather do than to have His children share the fullness of His power, provided we really believe that God will do that. Jesus shows us sharply and clearly the cause of our inward need and of our confusion, namely, that we never fully and convincingly believe that God is really ready and willing to make us new creatures.

At this point I must bring a word to your remembrance from the Sermon on the Mount. Considered generally, the Sermon, we have observed, is spoken in the tone of command. The Sermon does, however, contain promises, and one of them runs as follows: "Blessed are they that hunger and thirst after righteousness: for they shall be filled" (Matt. 5:6).

That word "righteousness" comprises many elements, and one of them is undoubtedly the true renewal of life. However, in that word "righteousness" this renewal of life is seen from a very special point of view. We are not concerned here with renewal of life *an sich,* in itself. We are not concerned with how we can get rid of those annoying sins, nor with how we can be delivered from the weariness of life which is inseparably connected with our character sins.

The word "righteousness" looks at the matter from God's point of view. We are here concerned with just one thing, namely, our affinity and kinship to God and with directing our lives in the proper relationship to Him. Righteousness is a conception devised by God. It does not place man in the center of things, but rather begins with God and our attitude toward Him. He who hungers and thirsts after that righteousness shall be filled.

But precisely here we must be careful. We feel bowed down under the weight of our egoism and our evil desires, and we long for deliverance. We really want moral rehabilitation. And we even seek it, because we know too well that unless we have it, we eventually will become the victims of a veritable chaos. But that surely is not the right motive for calling upon God. I am not saying that Jesus would not help a man who thus came to Him. In such a motive, however, no matter how reasonable it may be, there is a very strong element of egoism.

There is only one right and true motive, namely, the wish to be near unto God and to live with Him in the right relationship. We must "hunger and thirst," which means there must be a cry in our hearts and a thirst that cannot be quenched unless it is gratified.

We have brought to bear upon our inward needs the words of Jesus. We must remember that they are *His* words; *we* hardly know any longer what to say. We Christians of today have come to a deadlock. People ask us, Is there a way of complete deliverance, of being freed from those chaotic powers that spell our doom? We cannot answer the question. We can concoct theories, but inwardly we are convinced that we have reached an impasse. We have listened to beautiful sermons, enjoyed and admired them, but we have gone home and remained the same egoists we always were. There was no jarring and shaking, no disruption of our daily lives. We failed to see a change. We discovered that we were blind, that we were hateful as others are hateful, that we were dishonest as others are dishonest, and the image of Christ seemed blurred before our eyes.

And now that a whirlwind of destruction has come upon the world round about us, we have awakened. And we have come to ask the question, Is it really possible to live the Christian life, to live it in a different form and in a greater intensity than we have ever known? Is

Jesus Christ, who carried our sins and guilt on the Cross
and who has reconciled us to God, really able to deliver
us from the evil demon of our daily sins?

To these questions *Jesus* gives an answer. Yes, He
says, provided you embrace the truth, provided you
sharply examine the truth of your quest for salvation and
the infinite love of God, and hold on to that truth and
that love. It is possible, if you stop cherishing illusions
about yourselves and stop soothing and pacifying yourselves with all kinds of nonsense. Yes, it is, Christ says,
if you really *want* deliverance and if your desire is not
only a sudden flush and impulse but a complete, genuine,
and daily willingness. Yes, He says, provided you firmly
and surely believe that your Heavenly Father with open
arms will release for you the unlimited powers of the
Holy Spirit. Yes, provided you not only are concerned
to be delivered from that troublesome and annoying thing
that you call sin, but earnestly desire to live again in a
right relationship with God.

And if that is so, Christ says, I stand with you and
behind you. Then I am ready to help you all the way,
until you overcome triumphantly. Then I will make you
really free. Then you can depend on Me completely.
Then there is not a fairy-tale deliverance, which none of
us believes, but a deliverance which is true and real and
full.

REPENTANCE

We have listened to Jesus and have heard what He
has to say about the problems of our time. It is well
that we now return to ourselves and to the common,
everyday things of life.

I have looked around in the Church and I have found

people there for whom I have an unfeigned respect, strong, refined, and purified men, in whose lives I have discovered something of the saving power of the Lord Jesus Christ. I have seen men in whom, day after day, it is evident that they have been delivered, that they have been freed from the bonds of egoism and from the cravings of evil desires. To be sure, all those evil forces are still present in their lives, but there also is a true and real deliverance. They are different, and they have made more progress on the way of sanctification than others, and I thank God that in these tragic and terrible times in which we live many of His children receive grace and strength for great suffering and even for martyrdom. That encourages me when sometimes I am inclined to say in my haste, "All men are liars" (Ps. 116:11).

When, however, I observe Christianity as a whole and note how the mass of Christians live and think, I am often weighed down with a feeling of disappointment. I would say that we all have this experience again and again. We have moments of real and true longing to be delivered from the things that hold us in bondage, but every time we fall back into the old sins. We again indulge in slander; we again sink back into that subtle egoism, without even being aware of it, and again it poisons our minds. Now and then we rattle and shake our fetters, but we do not break and shatter them. We pray and pray to God, earnestly and pleadingly, to deliver us from the evil one. However, it is as if the heavens are of brass, as if our pleadings do not reach Him who alone can deliver us, as if our voice does not go beyond the reaches of our own heart.

In the majority of the Christians of our day we find a complete defeatism with regard to sin. They are discouraged, powerless, engulfed, and robbed of all confidence in the possibility of a real renewal of life. And when sometimes a great movement comes into being that aims to help man forward on the way of deliverance, and it appears that this movement fails to achieve its aim and purpose, a secret feeling of joy enters our hearts, and things again become as of old. We do not even realize that with this feeling we clearly show that in our lives we have swallowed disillusion, and that this makes us harsh and bitter.

Following Christ has disappointed us. We had expected much, infinitely much more. When for the first time our eyes were opened in the full consciousness of His grace, we imagined that it would be a very easy thing to serve such a Savior. We thought it would be an easy matter to forsake our sinful ways for His sake and to walk in His footsteps. Reality, however, has taught us differently. The enemies that we had been led to believe were dead, have begun to renew the attacks and have become stronger by the day, and He who would help us seems far off and difficult to reach. A mood of weariness has taken hold of us.

Jesus says: "So is the kingdom of God, as if a man should cast seed upon the earth; and should sleep and rise night and day, and the seed should spring up and grow, he knoweth not how" (Mark 4:26, 27).

No, we say, that is not true! The seed does *not* grow of itself; it does not grow at all! Growth does not come automatically. But when we say that, there is only one explanation, namely, that we are rebellious and do not give the seed a chance to grow because we do not want it to grow.

Where, then, do we fail? What is the real cause of our impotence, an impotence so profound that it dims our faith in the power of Jesus to give us deliverance?

When I put these questions, three answers occur to me, and I will name them.

First of all, this impotence is caused by our common loneliness and estrangement.   By this I mean that we all have become used to living as solitary beings.   And we consider it the most natural thing in the world.   In our attitude toward God we are self-contained; we keep to ourselves.   And we have a feeling that God merely allows us to drudge along in this world, and takes no notice at all of our difficulties and miseries.   We are also estranged from each other.   We do not allow another to look into our problems.   We do not share our defeats.   All the way we grapple and wrestle and struggle alone with our problems, with the result that we become deadly tired.

Years ago I heard a sermon that dealt with three texts, and those three texts remain with me till this day.   The first text was: "For each man shall bear his own burden" (Gal. 6:5).   The second text was: "Bear ye one another's burdens" (Gal. 6:2).   The third text was: "Casting all your care [anxiety, ASV] upon him" (I Pet. 5:7).

These three texts speak to the three aspects of our Christian life.   Everyone has to carry the burden of his own responsibility and of the choice he daily has to make.   Further, we should bear each other's burdens, namely, the burdens of cares and disappointments.   And we must cast all our burdens on the strong shoulders of Him who stands at our side.

Of these three texts we understand the first one very well, and we have concentrated on it.   We have become burden carriers *ad infinitum*.   We wage a grim battle against our evil desires, and we toil like blind men to transform our lives.   But we do not join together in

the fight against evil. We give each other too little or
no support. Above all, we do not go to God with our
disturbing troubles and cares, with our lusterless lives
full of trifles but very little glory. We do not have a
sufficient awareness that He stands back of us. We do
not understand Christ's parables, although in our superfici-
ality we think they are very easy to understand. We do
not understand that the Kingdom of Heaven has to grow
of itself, just as any seed, and that it will grow if only
we will not turn the things of the Kingdom into abstract
problems. We do not feel ourselves strongly held by
the powerful hand of God, and we therefore cannot understand that piety and devotion annoys and disturbs the
enemy, no matter how great and strong his realm may be.

A second cause of our impotence is our common unbelief. We do not believe that deliverance really is
possible. We say, and correctly so, that we shall remain
sinners until death, and that in this life we shall never
become entirely free from sin. We have learned, and
correctly so, that even the greatest saints have only a
very small beginning in perfect obedience. But this
does not mean that a change for the better is excluded and
impossible! It certainly does not mean that now we cannot change any more from glory unto glory! It does not
mean that Jesus is not able to free them who are slaves
to sin!

We have belittled ourselves, not realizing that in doing
so we have begun to belittle Jesus. We have not understood that we are well advanced in a retreat behind the
protecting walls of our own insignificance, quietly confident that thus we may remain our old self. And when
there is someone in our midst who courageously tries to
follow Christ, we disparage his attempts, gleeful that he
too will eventually meet great disappointment.

It is urgently necessary for all of us to say to each other that Jesus has the power to deliver men and women and young people from the slavery of lustful desires that drag our lives to dangerous and fatal depths. These desires may still surprise and overtake us, but Christ is able to give us complete deliverance. And He will also enable us to recognize our sins, and work in our hearts a real remorse and repentance. He has the power really to deliver us from such sins as self-esteem, self-sufficiency, being carried away with envy and jealousy, and remaining admirers and seekers of self even in the most noble things.

I do not believe that in this life we ever shall become perfect. Neither do I say that Christ has ever promised this. But He *has* promised that when a man has committed sin and discovers that he has become a slave of that sin, and embraces the truth, He will make him really free. And this I do not say. He has said that *Himself!*

The third cause of our impotence is our common unwillingness. When we are asked whether we wish to be healed, we often come along with the old answer: "Yes, Lord — but not yet!"

We have loved and cherished our faults altogether too much. We have become accustomed to a way of life in which all the insincerities and mutual irritations have become settled and anchored, and now we are averse to a change. We have become anchored to the moorings of our common mistakes. We have been seized and held in the grip of our errors, so that we ourselves do not even know how it could be different. Our conversation has become hollow. Our prayers have become impoverished and lame. Our society is full of discord and personal touchiness, so that often it seems wisest to remain at a proper distance from each other.

And we really do not wish for a change. We have accepted the situation; we have fully acquiesced. Even the thought of what would have to happen to bring about a change, oppresses us. And round about us is the world, full of hatred and war, with its nameless misery, with its anxieties and dangers. We no longer know how to bring the good news. When we say that the truth will make us free, we are afraid that someone will confront *yes* us with the question: "But you, are you free?"

I see very clearly that the figure of Jesus Christ stands above all the needs of our time, and that He alone can help us. But I hesitate to boast, because I am afraid that, deep in my heart, there will be the acid smile of hardly believing myself what I preach to others.

Still I dare say that Jesus Christ is able to set free a person who is bound in slavery, because I have heard *Him* say that. I know that it is true, and He has let us see it in the lives of "the cloud of witnesses" who surround us. I know that it is true, and when finally we shall awake and shall rise from the dead, the brightness of His face will lighten and illuminate us. And I also know that together we shall then find the right way of walking in the way of His promises.

And I still dare to say, be it shamefacedly: "There is forgiveness with Thee, that Thou mayest be feared. And with Thee there is mercy and plenteous redemption."

Free, really free, as Jesus has said! A longing wells up in our hearts, a real yearning to be delivered from our *yes* misery.